NORWEGIAN HISTORY
SIMPLIFIED

Zinken Hopp

NORWEGIAN HISTORY SIMPLIFIED

Translated by Toni Ramholt

John Griegs Forlag

Printed in Norway by
A.s John Griegs Boktrykkeri, Bergen

This little book does not pretend to be history as taught in school by a teacher familiar with all the dates. Neither is it a highly coloured narrative, intended solely for entertainment. It is a simple account of some of the facts an intelligent and observant traveller to our country needs to know when he sees our ancient monuments, studies our daily life and possibly wonders a little about our national traditions, or even sometimes the lack of them.

History can be told in many ways, and I have chosen to tell it through the medium of things we consider especially Norwegian — our historical heritage, so to speak, and I shall attempt to describe the events and circumstances which produced them. When a traveller comes across the statue of one of our great men, it is natural for him to wish to know something about him, and I shall do my best, without trying to be another Baedeker, to satisfy his curiosity.

Our forbears called their country Norvegr, which we have shortened to Norge. It means simply "the way to the North" — or Norway. We figure in European history as the people from the North, and it is as such we regard ourselves to this day. Hammerfest, the most northerly town in the world, is in Norway. Where the North Cape, northernmost bastion of Europe, plunges its masses into the vast Arctic Ocean, Norwegians live and work and make their homes. "The warm currents of seawater which come to us from the Gulf of Mexico make our coasts habitable farther north than in other lands". This is the first sentence in our geography text-book.

The Vikings came from the North in ancient times, — hairy barbarians who crossed the North Sea in their long ships, dragon-heads at the prow, to plunder in England and France. From the North too came the Varangians who found their way as far south as Constantinople where they served as the Emperor's bodyguard and were much admired for their broad shoulders and fair hair.

And it was from the far North that Ottar the Viking came sailing to the court of Alfred the Great, bringing with him walrus tusks and other strange merchandise. He gave an account of a voyage up the coast of Norway, round the North Cape into the White Sea. King Alfred had his scribe record these travels on parchment, and Ottar's experiences were later included in the Anglo-Saxon translation of Orosius' History of the World.

But Norway had her own history long before that time. It has been said that history begins when a people leaves behind its first monumental inscriptions, and the area of our country is so extensive that these simple tracings from the hands of our forefathers have to a great extent been left undisturbed. Our ancestors were hunters who lived off the fish in the sea and the game in the forest, and here as in other lands, pictures are found of their quarry. We have no caves in our craggy mountains, where the Norseman could decorate his dwelling as other races have done in France and Spain. His animal tracings are carved on the solid rock face at watering places where big game came to drink, or by steep cliffs where the reindeer could be driven over to their death. Many of these images are vividly drawn, most of them life-size or even larger. But whatever colour they may once have had has disappeared long ago.

They are, unfortunately, by no means easy of access. Some of them are almost inaccessible, for they were not intended for exhibition. We are not always sure of their significance, but they were certainly not meant for the entertainment of the casual passer-by. However, on the Bardal farm at Steinkjer, on the Trondheim Fjord, anyone can see, without much effort, the great elks carved on the surface of the rock.

Animal images of this kind are found mainly in Northern Norway, but one artist has been considerate enough to place his within easy reach of

7

Oslo, at Ekeberg. It is not difficult to find, fenced in and marked out as it is, but by no means easy to distinguish, for it is a rather poor specimen, both technically and artistically. If the light is good, one can just make out the contours of reindeer on the rock surface, at the place where our skin-clad fore-fathers lay in wait for their kill.

We can truly call these people our forefathers, for Norway has never been conquered by foreign races since the Ice Age, when the great glaciers melted and people came to settle on our coasts and in our forests. These early settlers were of various tribes, evidence of which can still be seen in the different racial strains in our country today: for instance, the round-skulled Alpine race in the south, and the Lapps, a small minority, in the far north. But after these first immigrants, no other races came to share the land with them, and that is why Norwegians have so strong a feeling of owning their country and belonging to it.

Our ancestors roasted their meat over outdoor fires in the summer and on primitive hearths in their huts in the winter. They killed their enemies, hunted game, fished, reproduced their species. The many flint objects they left about — fish-hooks and such like — together with the remains of their feasts, have earned the gratitude of archaeologists.

The people of the next age, the Bronze Age, have left even more interesting relics, for they too carved images in the steep mountain sides. But these were very different from the earlier tracings, for these people covered the rocky surfaces with pictures of little men, ships, weapons, circles and crosses. It is evident that they had important messages to convey, but  they are certainly not easy to interpret. We believe them to be chiefly religious symbols, and obviously the cult of the sun god prevailed, for the sun motif is repeatedly used.

Anyone can see these pictures for himself, for some are preserved in our museums, while others are still in their original positions and can be found in great numbers along the roads between Fredrikstad on the south coast and the Swedish frontier. Some of these Bronze Age pictures are carved beside, or even on top of, the older tracings of animals, as at Bardal, near Steinkjer, mentioned above.

We have now reached the Iron Age and, far south in the Mediterranean, Rome has become a world power. While it has never been proved that the Romans visited us, or vice versa, we do know that Pytheas, the Greek, sailed to a country he called Thule — but whether this was Norway or Denmark is doubtful. The Romans called the unexplored North Ultima Thule, but Ptolemaios on his map of the world in the year 150 indicated Norway only as an undefined white patch, although he has Denmark clearly marked. Meanwhile, here in the

North the people settled in groups and chose their kings: a religious faith took shape, and customs developed into laws. As yet no single name emerges, and true history cannot dawn until one man, by reason of his qualities, stands out from his fellow men. But already important events and names must have been handed down from man to man. It is curious to note that while the Roman Empire had already passed its zenith, our land was still shrouded in obscurity.

The centuries rolled on their way .... In the long winter evenings, gathered around the open hearth, the wise old folk retold tales of their grandfathers, and the lively young people composed songs around these themes. It was said that the great gods had once lived on earth in human guise. Odin, the Mighty, driven out of Germany by the Roman legions, had made his way northwards and settled with all his kindred in Uppsala in Sweden. Odin was the wisest of all gods, and the god of combat. All his sons too were gods, and peace and prosperity prevailed in his time. But the gods died and passed to another realm where Odin now reigns and watches over the fate of mankind with his one remaining eye — the other having been bartered for the gift of wisdom. His sons lived and died as human beings, only on a grander scale, and after death were translated to Aasgaard, the home of the gods. The last of the race of gods on earth was the fair Freya, goddess of fertility. But according to legend, men sprang from the loin of gods, and the Norse chieftains proudly claimed to be their descendants.

Among the kings in Uppsala, offspring of the gods, Fjolne is the first name to appear in our sagas. He was a mighty king, but he died a strange death while on a visit to the King of Denmark. A huge vat to hold mead had been made for the occasion, and during the night, having to leave his bed for natural reasons, Fjolne fell into this vat and was drowned. His curious fate made a deep impression on his contemporaries, and ballads were composed about "the Sea King who sank in the windless waves". For already at that time Nordic poets had developed their peculiar talent for metaphor, and some intelligence was required to interpret their lyrics, the declamation of which became a kind of guessing game for the listeners.

Many kings were descended from Fjolne, the son of Frey, god of fertility. They had wealth as well as courage, but their kin was dogged by ill luck from the day the brothers Gisl and Ondur bade the witch Huld cast a spell over their treacherous father, King Domalde. Huld promised to do so, but warned them that her black magic would have fearful results in the form of strife and sudden death. However, the King's two young sons persisted, for their hatred of their father dominated them to the exclusion of all else. Huld did her worst, and famine swept the land. No sacrifice could appease the gods and cause the corn to grow. Finally, as the very last resort, the subjects of King Domalde took the drastic step of offering their king as a human sacrifice, and from that time, for all except the king's kindred, there was peace and plenty in the land.

The bards recited their lays, mostly of bold men who risked their lives and died with stoic calm. Even the vilest man deserved respect for a splendid death — and who more than King Ingjald and his daughter Aase? He was a blackguard all his life, promising mercy to twelve kings and going back on his word. Ingjald the Evil was the name he was given, and the same name followed his daughter Aase who caused the death of both her own brother and her husband. When retribution finally overtook the King and his daughter and the enemy approached, they recognised the inevitable, made all their men dead drunk and set fire to the house — perishing in the flames.

Motifs of this kind have had great significance in our art and literature when the great wave of national romanticism set in towards the end of the last century. This drawing is by Gerhard Munthe, (1840—1929), as it appears in the issue of Snorre's Saga of the Kings in 1899.

This royal dynasty to which Queen Aase belonged was called the Yngling family, and came to Norway from Sweden. Rulers over small kingdoms in the east country around the Oslo Fjord boasted of their descent from the gods of Uppsala.

From this dim saga background of fire and bloodshed emerge two figures of authentic historical interest — sons of the same father, but by different mothers. They are Olav and Halvdan, two Viking kings of great importance to their country, but in very different ways.

Of the eldest, Olav, the saga tells us that his domain lay to the west of Oslo Fjord and was of no great size. But he was king and gained a reputation for great daring both on land and sea. His seat was at Geirstad, and he is known as Olav Geirstad-Alv. Taller than most men, and handsomer, he died of a disease in a leg, and his men buried him on his own ground and, as the custom was, covered the grave with a large burial-mound.

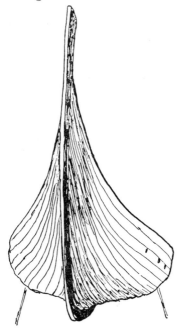

Poems in his honour still tell of the valiant king who lay under the mound by the fjord.

A thousand years later, our archaeologists uncovered his ship, buried with him in the mound, and found it still in good condition. The place was now called Gokstad and the ship is, therefore, known as the Gokstad ship. Here was proof that the sagas spoke the truth and that Olav *was* taller than most men; and a fine figure of a man he must have been until arthritis crippled him.

We cannot go into detail here about the Gokstad ship, but anyone who knows about sailing can see that it was a fine ship, and readers of the sagas will rejoice over this scientific confirmation of their truthfulness.

Olav Geirstad-Alv's ship constitutes a real cultural monument, not only as a lasting illustration of our sagas, but also as a proof of our early skill in shipbuilding. In 1893, an exact replica of the Gokstad ship was built and a Norwegian seaman, Magnus Andersen, went aboard with his crew. With the exception of a compass, they had no other aids to navigation than the Vikings themselves had. Admittedly, the Vikings also used a kind of compass, but a very primitive one — a lodestone, which was a magnetic oxide of iron. The first Vikings to cross the Atlantic may or may not have had a lodestone to guide them, but Skipper Andersen took a compass with him, to be on the safe side. In many ways he and his crew were better equipped than the ancient Vikings, but the oars and the sails were certainly no better. The

"Viking" crossed the Atlantic, the wind in her striped sail, without mishaps of any kind.

From Olav's brother, Halvdan, came a heritage of a different kind. He was the offspring of a marriage which can hardly have been harmonious, for his father Gudroed the Hunter, had taken his wife Aase by force and killed her father and brother before her eyes. Before the child Halvdan was one year old, Queen Aase had sent her bondsman to kill the King, her husband. (Bear in mind the name Aase — we shall return to her later!).

This Halvdan the Swart is the founder of our royal dynasty. He is a proud figure in Norwegian history, a man who made laws and kept them himself, a man whom Fortune smiled upon and, best of all, in whose shadow the corn grew high and the live-stock thrived. His consort, the fair Ragnhild, dreamed one night that she removed a thorn from the hem of her gown, and the thorn took root and became a mighty tree, with branches stretching across the whole of Norway. Wise men nodded sagely when they heard this strange dream and interpreted it to mean that her progeny would rule over the whole kingdom.

Ragnhild and Halvdan the Swart had a son, Harald by name, who became king while still a boy. One day, when he had grown to manhood, he heard of a beautiful maiden called Gyda and sent his messengers to ask her to be his wife. The proud Gyda answered that she had no intention of giving herself to anybody but a great king, ruler of all Norway. Now, chivalry to women was not a prominent quality of the Vikings, and many of his men thought Harald ought to give Gyda a good beating for her arrogance. But Harald was of another opinion: he accepted her decision and swore not to cut or comb his hair until he had conquered his enemies. He progressed from valley to valley and was accepted by the minor kings as their overlord, although not always without a clash of arms. His warriors ("berserks" they are called in our tongue, from the bear-skin they wore) fought **872** fiercely on land and at sea, until at the final battle at Hafrsfjord, near Stavanger, they met the combined fleet of several minor kings and outmanoeuvred them. Harald was now sovereign lord of Norway. At last his hair could be cut: it had become so long and thick during these years of struggle, that he has gone down to history as Harald Fairhair. The proud Gyda became his wife, one of many. He had a long life and bred many sons, and his end was peaceful, for he died in his bed — an unusual occurrence in those days. Harald came from the broad fertile valleys of the east, but he chose as his last resting-place a spot near Haugesund on the west coast, ravaged by storms and gales. The great stone block of his own choice lies there still, covering his grave, and in 1872, on the 1000th anniversary of the great day when the land of the Norsemen became one united kingdom, a stone monument was raised to mark the place, according to the custom of the ancient Vikings in honouring their chieftains. Travellers who sail along the west coast of Norway on a fine summer's day can see this monument on the green hills north of Karmsund.

From now on, Norway has a documented history, complete with names and events, and we can form a fairly clear picture of how daily life was lived in our country and of the ideals which guided our forefathers.

You remember Queen Aase was mentioned above. It has never been proved, but seems likely that it was she who was buried with the Oseberg ship, excavated in 1904. The name itself means Aase's hill or mound. Two old women were buried there, one a queen, the other her faithful bonds-woman who died with her. Which of the two is the queen we do not know, for Death is a great leveller. Tools and utensils of all kinds lay in the ship as the custom was, for use after death, and they tell us of a practical hard-working people who gained their living from sea and land. Here were textiles which bore witness to a highly developed skill in weaving and sewing among the women, with de-signs of which the motifs were the fearful and the terrible. In those days people prided themselves upon their strength and courage, and in their art they portrayed — not gentle idylls, but visions of "the Morning of Time when eagles screamed over seething waters". Queen Aase was not made of the stuff that dreams of flowering meadows and gentle breezes. At the head of her bed were carved gaping monsters with 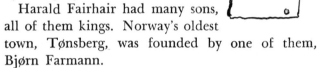 flickering venomous tongues, as was fitting for a Dowager Queen who had borne her son to a man who stole her, at the point of the sword, from her father's house, and upon whom she revenged herself by bringing about his death.

Harald Fairhair had many sons, all of them kings. Norway's oldest town, Tønsberg, was founded by one of them, Bjørn Farmann.

The most popular of Harald's sons was Haakon, who was brought up at the court of King Athelstan of England. The circumstances which brought this about give interesting glimpses of strategy of a kind which is unfortunately always with us, even if the details vary with the centuries. King Athelstan sent his emissaries to King Harald, with the gift of a sword. As the Norwegian king thanked them, he tried the sword in his hand, whereupon they informed him with a smile that according to English custom he had by his acceptance of the symbolic sword ackowledged Athelstan as his liege lord. King Harald, however, was not amused. He looked around him for a means of retaliation, and his eye fell upon one of his sons — a young boy named Haakon, whose mother was of low descent and whose birth had taken place under very unregal conditions; his mother began her labour while still on board the ship which was to take her to King Harald, and the crew had seen no other solution but to carry her ashore. And here on the bare rocks she had given birth to her son Haakon.

Harald now sent his men with the baby boy to King Athelstan in England, with the request that the child be brought up at the English court. When the king took the infant upon his knee the Norsemen laughed and said that now he was Harald's vassal, for according to Norwegian custom the sons of the overlord were brought up by his subjects. Athelstan, enraged, drew his sword to kill little Haakon, upon which the Vikings warned him that Harald had many more sons. To King Athelstan's credit, the boy was reared wisely and well as his foster son, and on the death of King **950** Harald he returned to his fatherland — a young man beautiful to behold, in a golden helmet and with a fine sword in his hand. The sword was called Kvernbit, for it could cleave millstones. The young Haakon tried to introduce into Norway the Christian faith in which he was brought up, but as he was told that this would cost him his life, he abandoned the attempt. The account of his death, some years later, is dramatic and moving, for, fatally wounded in battle, he requested his men to carry him ashore at the very place where he first saw the light of day. His crew asked if they should not sail to England and bury him in Christian soil, but Haakon spoke as a true Viking and declared that he had lived a heathen and must die a heathen.

He is remembered as Haakon the Good in Norway, for his rule was wise and farsighted. He organised the defence of the country, and established warning beacons, on the mountain tops, to be lit at the approach of alien ships. In this way, the whole of Norway's long coast could be in a state of preparedness within seven days.

The strongest of all Harald's sons was Erik Blood-Axe, who was driven out of his country and settled in Northumberland, with his headquarters at York.

We now come to Olav Tryggvason — a king who was the ideal of Norwegian men and women alike.
995 Fair and handsome, taller than other men, stronger than most, broad of shoulder, but slender. He climbed mountains where no man had set foot before, and he sailed the proudest ship of all — *Ormen Lange* ("The Long Serpent"). After a stormy youth spent plundering and fighting in Viking raids, he became a Christian and returned to his native land. He went ashore at Moster, an island off the west coast, where he knelt in prayer and swore to do everything in his power to introduce

Christianity into Norway. According to the saga, a church was built on the spot where he landed. The little stone church at Moster, still standing, is among the oldest in Norway.

He did succeed in establishing Christianity — by fair means and foul, mostly foul. The pagan sanctuaries were torn down and the effigies of the gods destroyed. Any treasure found there he confiscated. A large gold ring which he found in the door of one of these places of worship, he sent to the lady he was wooing at the time — the proud Queen Sigrid the Haughty of Sweden. She did what many a wordly-wise woman has done after her: she had it examined to discover its real value. When broken in two, sure enough it was found to contain a core of copper. Was King Olav aware of this, she asked herself? A woman cannot be too careful where gifts to tempt her are concerned. Queen Sigrid was still suspicious when they finally met, but she let Olav have his say and everything appeared to be going smoothly, until the King made one demand: that she should change her faith and become a Christian. To which she replied that for her part she intended to remain in the faith of her ancestors, whereas he could do as he pleased. King Olav, enraged, hit her in the face with his glove, declaring that he would never marry a heathen jade. Whereupon they both rose to their full height and Queen Sigrid uttered the ominous words: "This may well mean your destruction!"

Olav was not lucky in love. His first wife, whom he met on his travels, when young, chose to live and die on the shores of the Baltic. His second tried to kill him on their wedding night, in revenge for the execution of her father. His third was Tyra, a Danish princess, who had been married to the heathen King Burisleif of the Baltic lands. But she was discontented with Olav for not reclaiming her dowry, for fear of encountering her brother King Svein Forkbeard on the way. He could do but one thing to prove his worth as husband and king, and in the year 1000 he sailed southward with *The Long Serpent* manned by the finest body of men that had ever been mustered in Norway. One of them, the 18-year old Einar Tambarskjelve, was a better bowman even than the King himself.

Having collected his wife's inheritance, Olav sailed north again, and was then attacked by the combined fleets of the Danish and the Swedish kings — the latter urged on by Queen Sigrid — together with the Norwegian petty chieftains in **1000** revolt against Olav. The battle was joined at Svolder, in the Baltic, and never have men fought more fiercely. Whomsoever Einar shot at with his great bow was killed instantly. At the height of the fray, an arrow hit Einar's bow and it snapped with a loud noise. "What broke so loudly?", shouted the King. "Norway out of your hand, Sire!", Einar's reply came back to him through the clamour of the battle. The odds were hopelessly against them, and rather than surrender, Olav and his warriors jumped overboard, preferring death by drowning. Einar Tambarskjelve survived and lived to enjoy a ripe old age, honoured by all.

It is likely that a foreigner might have difficulties with the pronunciation of Olav Tryggvason's name, but in our ears it resounds like martial music and the clash of blows on shields. His statue you will find in Trondheim, the town he founded. He stands proudly on top of a column in the heart of the city where all can admire his fine physique.

The next great man in our history is Olav the Holy — the most important of them all. He continued the work of conversion to Christianity and after a stormy reign of 15 years, he was obliged to flee to Sweden. In a heroic attempt to win his country back, he fell in the battle of Stiklestad, near Trondheim.

1015—30

Hardly was the King dead before a great change in the religious climate of Norway set in, and those who had previously opposed Olav with every means in their power, now acknowledged their fault. Olav was declared a saint, and his shrine in Trondheim became a centre of devotion for the whole country. His name is famous in our history, and Olav is still the most popular boy's name we have. Our national coat-of-arms shows a lion holding an axe in its paws — the weapon Olav bore the day he was slain. The highest decoration any Norwegian can gain is called the Order of St. Olav.

Legend has spun a fine web of mysticism around his name, and in many of our churches and museums are old pictures of him which have been the object of great devotion. Pilgrims from the whole of Northern Europe visited the church built over his grave in Trondheim — a church so large and splendid that to this very day it fills us with wonder and awe. Churches built in his honour can still be found in Denmark and Sweden — and also in England, where his name was held in great esteem. Once there were 15 churches dedicated to St. Olav in England alone, apart from those in the Orkneys and the Shetlands. One still stands in Kirkwall, another in London — where the name of Tooley Street commemorates him, for the name St. Olav became distorted either to St. Holofius or to Tooley.

It may amuse our readers to note that the text of this children's ditty may possibly have a connection with our St. Olav. It begins:

"London Bridge is falling down, falling down, falling down,

London Bridge is falling down, my fair lady",
and goes on:

"So we dance in Tooley Street, Tooley Street, Tooley Street,

so we dance in Tooley Street — my fair lady".

In Tooley Street was the Church of St. Olav, but what had he to do with London Bridge? He pulled it down — yes, he actually *did pull it down!*

St. Olavs figure still stands in Lübeck, a crown on his head and an axe in his hand, the dragon of heathendom writhing under his foot.

His men fastened ropes around the piles upon which the bridge rested, and rowed with all their might away from it — until London Bridge collapsed. But this was in the days of reckless youth, before his sorrows began.

In Fritwell in Oxfordshire there still is (or at least there was in 1930) a little church bearing the name of St. Olav, where every year, on August the 8th, a service is held in his memory. In the Red Book of Derby, written in 1060, where the names of all saintly men are inscribed, Olav is the only one not born and bred in the British Isles. A chapel was built to his honour in Constantinople in the Middle Ages. In Rome today there is an altar dedicated to him, and his picture, painted in the 13th century, hangs to this day in the Church of Our Lady in Bethlehem.

So great was the fame of St. Olav that the Hanseatic merchants from Northern Germany, who annexed the profitable trade in Norway towards the end of the Middle Ages, chose St. Olav as their patron and protector in their task of exploiting the land.

In Norway St. Olav lives on in saga and legend. If a sound is very narrow or the shores unusually steep, it is because St. Olav sailed right through the mountain in his ship. A mark resembling a horse's hoof in the solid rock is sure to be the imprint of St. Olav's charger, a cleft in a boulder by the church-wall the place where he plunged his spear.

Although his downfall was caused rather by his politics than by his religion, yet posterity proclaims him a martyr for his faith, and the day of his death is celebrated annually as the triumph of Christianity in Norway.

After Olav's death the powerful King Canute of **1035—47** England and Denmark had most influence in the government of our country, but it was not long before Olav's son Magnus became king. In the sagas he is given the title of Magnus the Good, and he is the generally accepted model for Prince Fortinbras who makes such an effective entry in the last scene of "Hamlet". For young Magnus was also ruler of Denmark during his short life. He was a noble young man who truly deserved his cognomen. The name of Magnus he received in a curious way. He was born in the night and, fearing that both mother and child would die, the priests advised the immediate baptism of the infant. None dared to wake the King, for he hated to have his sleep disturbed. Sigvat the Skald, the King's court poet, declared that he would rather name the boy himself than incur the King's anger by waking him at dead of night. The name he chose was Magnus. The following morning the King was informed of the birth of a son who, contrary to expectations, lived, and bore a name unheard before in Norway. Olav rebuked Sigvat for his presumption, but the poet retorted that he dared not let a soul depart this life unbaptised, and the name he had chosen was borrowed from the Emperor Carolus Magnus (Charlemagne). The King was pacified and soon found he liked the name, as his fellow countrymen have done ever since. The curious thing here is that Sigvat was mistaken, for the Emperor's actual name was Carolus, and Magnus (i. e. Great) an additional complimentary designation.

The next in the line of kings was Olav's brother, Harald Hardrada, a strong-willed man and a severe **1046–66** taskmaster, but a capable regent and a gifted poet. To him Earl Toste came from England to beg for help against his brother Harald Godwinson, and Harald Hardrada was not the man to neglect such an opportunity. A fleet was fitted out and the

Norsemen went ashore in England and plundered the land in true Viking style. King Harald Godwinson rode to meet them with a force outnumbering the Norsemen many times and the sagas **1066** give a most graphic description of their clash at Stamford Bridge.

Twenty men rode out from the English army, both men and mounts clad in chainmail, and when they came within earshot of the Norwegian raiders one of them called: "Is Earl Toste among you?" Toste himself replied: "You'll find him here!" Then the horseman said: "Harald, your brother, sends greetings and offers you the whole of Northumberland and a third of his kingdom". Earl Toste replied: "Had this offer come earlier, many men would have been alive today and the kingdom of England would have been better off. If I accept, what will my friend Harald from Norway get for his trouble?" The answer came: "Seven feet of English ground, or as much more as he is taller than other men!" "Then", said the Earl, "go back to your ranks and prepare for battle. Never shall the Norsemen say with truth that Earl Toste abandoned Harald Hardrada to the enemy when they went to fight side by side in England. Upon this we are all resolved, either to die with honour or to gain England by victory". At these words the horsemen turned and rode back to their ranks. The Norwegian King turned to his ally and asked who the eloquent fellow was. "That was King Harald Godwinson". Harald was enraged and

Harald Hardrada rides proudly on the facade of Oslo Town Hall, for it was he who founded our present capital.

asked why he had not been told before: "He was so close and he should never have been allowed to carry back the tidings of our men's slaughter". "True indeed", answered Toste, "but he came to offer me peace and much land, and I would sooner he be my murderer than I his'. Harald Hardrada turned to his men and said: "He was but a little man, yet he sat firmly in his saddle". They were almost his last words, for he fell in the battle, his throat pierced by an arrow, and Harald Godwinson was the victor. This was only a few weeks before the bloody battle of Hastings, where a more powerful conqueror, William of Normandy, vanquished the Anglo-Saxon army.

You will notice that Oslo has rather a remark-

able coat-of-arms: it represents in a simplified form the events leading up to the death of St. Hallvard. The young Hallvard was a high-born man, the King's cousin, and he met his fate one day when he pushed his boat out to row across the fjord to his father's property. A poor old woman came running to the shore, calling to him for help, for she was accused of theft and three men were persuing her to kill her. Hallvard took her into his boat and rowed for dear life, but the three men overtook him and commanded him to give up the woman. Hallvard questioned them and decided that her guilt was not proven, upon which the three vengeful men became enraged and one of them shot an arrow which killed the chivalrous young man. The murderers tied a millstone round his neck and sank the body in the fjord, while the old woman was beaten to death and buried ashore. But Hallvard's body floated up and he was declared a saint by popular acclaim. He is depicted with a millstone in one hand, three arrows in the other and a woman at his feet. He is the patron saint of Oslo bishopric, and the town of Drammen, which lies close to his father's property, has raised to his memory a fine monument, where he stands as the central figure of a splendid fountain.

Harald Hardrada had a son, Olav Kyrre, a man

of peace who loved the good things of life and, what is rarer, deserved them too. It was he who **1066—93** founded Bergen.

Olav Kyrre's son was Magnus, who was given the strange nickname of Barefoot. He was a wild young man who lived according to his motto that "Kings are made for honour, not for long life". Magnus was the last Viking king of Norway, the last to sail westwards to raid the coasts of the British Isles and set up vassal states there. He fell **1103** in a battle in Ulster, and Irish folksongs and ballads record his death.

The Viking Age had come to an end, and what was to show for all the daring sea-voyages and raids? What had Norsemen learned from others? Had other races learned anything from their plunderers? Let us look at the results:

Iceland had been populated. The Vikings found this land deserted and barren, and many of them settled there and made it their home. Together with others of Irish and Scottish descent they formed a new nation remarkable for its narrative powers and ability to preserve old legends and writings. Our debt to Iceland in this respect is incalculable, for without the literary heritage from Iceland we should be poor indeed — and not Norway alone but the whole of Northern Europe.

In their good seaworthy ships, the Vikings had sailed even as far as America. They called it Vinland, and Eirik the Red and Leif Eiriksson founded the first European settlements on North American soil. But they were unable to maintain this territory, and the sailing route was forgotten. There were Norse settlers in Greenland, and the inhabitants of the Orkneys, the Shetlands and the Faroe Islands were subject to the King of Norway.

In England and Ireland the Vikings were firmly established. They contributed to the racial diversity in the British Isles, where place names still proclaim a Norwegian origin. The city of York, the experts say, takes its name from a Viking settlement called Jorvik, and there are many such examples. After the Norman Conquest in 1066, no more is heard of Scandinavian raids in England.

While the Swedes gained a foothold in Russia and ventured as far south as Constantinople, the Danes and Norwegians joined forces and plundered the verdant land of France, which must have seemed to them an earthly paradise, inhabited by craven men and well-fed cattle. The French called the Viking leader Rollo. The Danes claim him for their own, but Norwegian history asserts that he was a Norwegian named Gange-Rolv ("the Walker") because he was of such a size that no horse could bear his weight. Our sagas reveal that he was the black sheep of an otherwise respectable family, that he was banished by Harald Fairhair and fled to France where he conquered the territory now known as Normandy, the land of the Norsemen. Here he became a chieftain, with the title of Duke. The history of his family is incom-

The town of Rouen has recognised Rollo as Norwegian, and presented his statue to the town of Aalesund, the home of his ancestors. He looks a true adventurer, as travellers to Aalesund can see for themselves.

plete, but as far as we can tell it was his great-great-grandson William who conquered England in 1066.

During the Viking Age, Norsemen had established their place in Europe. We were then, and have remained, a seafaring nation. Small wonder that ships have always been dear to our hearts, and that this symbol can be found on many objects of art throughout the centuries.

Our clothing in the Middle Ages was influenced by English customs and fashions from the time of the Viking invasions. This fact is mentioned in our sagas. Christianity was now firmly established in our land, and in its wake came books and the Latin language and its alphabet. This did not mean that the indigenous form of writing, the runic signs, at once fell into disuse. These had been adapted, far back in history, from the alpha-

ᚠᚢᚦᚨᚱᚴ : ᚼᚾᛁᛅᛋ : ᛏᛒᚤᛚᛙ

f u th ø r k h n i a s t b m l n

bet in use in the Mediterranean area. The runic signs were best suited for carving in wood and were used for this purpose before paper was in general use.

The old decorative style used by the Vikings in wood carving and metal work was now gradually replaced by European Romanesque designs. Yet we still admire the complicated entwined patterns on the Vikings' weapons and decorated ornaments. In our days, old buckles have been copied for use with our modern clothes, and we find them eminently suitable.

From the beginning of the 12th century we have our share in the general development of Europe

1103–30 — not as pirates and robbers, but as allies of the other Christian princes. Our next king, Sigurd Jorsalfarer, set off for the Crusades while his brother Eystein remained to reign in his stead. In those days the law decreed that any of the King's sons might become king, if he were

bold enough to demand this right, legitimate or not. So far this arrangement had worked well, and the strong and boisterous Sigurd lived on a reasonably good footing with the gentle Eystein, except when they both drank too deep a draught of mead at table and quarrelled loudly, to the delight of their listening henchmen.

Of all the buildings that good King Eystein erected, the only one to survive intact is the beautiful St. Mary's Church in Bergen, miraculously saved from the numerous fires which have ravaged the town throughout the centuries.

The building of the stave-church at Garmo is mentioned in the saga of St. Olav. It has been enlarged
at a later date, and is now at Maihaugen, the open-
air museum at Lillehammer.

Even now, with the addition of portraits of stout
merchants from the 17th century, the church
still breathes the simple and devout spirit of a
distant age.

Having mentioned buildings, we must tell our
reader something about our most venerable monuments — the stave churches, very specially our own.

As could be expected from a nation of shipbuilders, Norwegians showed great skill in timber construction, such outstanding skill as to amaze and impress experts to this very day. The commonly used technique in the construction of large buildings was to raise a sturdy framework of vertical poles ("staves") and then fill in with vertical boards.  Later a simplified technique was practised, of placing the logs horizontally, the one upon the other, until the required height was reached and the roof could be laid. But for a church or a chieftain's hall the former type was used, with the timber columns pointing heavenwards, frequently with a double row in the mid-aisle.

The churches in the towns were as a rule built of stone, but in the country districts timber churches were erected throughout the Middle Ages. Of these pitch-covered stave churches, built of timber pillars and surrounded by an ambulatory surmounted by rooflets and spires, there are still a score or so existing to our day. The most beautiful of these were built in the time of Eystein and Sigurd and the wood carving shows the transition from the heathen influence to the inspiration of Romanesque ecclesiastical stone architecture. The traces found here of old Norse traditions are of profound interest to us, these capitals with the one-eyed man who can be no other than Odin, or mythical beasts who have no connection with Christendom.

The ancient gods still lived on in the people's imagination. They were the forces of Nature, governing the elements and the seasons, life and death. Honoured by saga and legend, they also made a more lyrical appearance in poetry. The creative inspiration of the old Nordic skalds was firmly rooted in heathen beliefs and could not be eradicated, for the images were rich and manifold in the sagas and their interpretation was frequently to be found in religious symbols. Nobody could understand that "Freya's tears" meant «gold» if they did not know that the goddess of love weeps tears of gold. These references are so numerous and so obscure that the old Norse lays are practically incomprehensible for the uninitiated. If they are translated directly, the meaning can frequently be made clear only by a series of footnotes, though at times they achieve an almost classic simplicity:

> *"Men rode by night,*
> *mailed hauberks.*
> *Shields shone*
> *'gainst the scarred moon".*

1130 After the death of King Sigurd, civil war broke out and lasted with intervals for 110 years. It was bound to come when, as already mentioned, all the King's sons, whether legitimate or illegitimate, had the right to become kings. As the kings were of the Viking breed, they were liable to die young, and many left a flock of turbulent sons. Anybody could proclaim himself the son of the King — if he had the courage and his mother supported his claim. The traditional method of proving the truth of this was to go through the ordeal of "jernbyrd". This meant either walking barefoot on red hot iron in church, or carrying glowing iron a prescribed number of steps, under the eyes of the priests. Whoever dared to call upon God to witness the validity of his claim would come through this trial by fire without a blemish.

But the actual position of these royal pretenders was complicated enough, for the strong political and clerical powers in the land would, moral grounds apart, support the claim that suited them best. Humanity changes but little in the course of the centuries.

The first of our kings during the Civil War was an Irishman, Harald Gillchrist by name. He claimed to be the son of Magnus Barefoot conceived during his raids in Ireland. He survived the "jernbyrd" ordeal unharmed, and so established his claim to the throne. But his reign was memorable only for violence and murder, until finally he in his turn was murdered in his bed. Two sons were born to him in Norway, Inge Hunchback and Sigurd Mouth, and they continued the struggle one against the other. To add to the confusion, an elder Scottish half-brother, Eystein, arrived to join the fight, but he was soon murdered by his Norwegian brothers.

This Scottish Eystein Haraldson had a son, so slight of build that he was called "the Maiden" (Eystein Meyla). This young man met his death at the battle of Re, near Tønsberg, in 1177. This battle made little difference to the wild erratic progress of the Civil War, but it is a date that Norwegian schoolchildren are expected to remember, for this is the last event recorded by Snorre Sturlasson in his famous Saga of the Kings.

Norsemen have always appreciated a good story-teller. They acknowledged the Icelanders as the finest of narrators and Snorre as the best of them all. Other saga-writers came after him, but none with his talent as an historian or his incomparable style.

Our Viking sagas chronicle the affairs of a state with a highly developed system of laws but no police force to uphold these laws. It was everybody's individual concern to see that he and his kin were not molested or dishonoured. The word *Vengeance* gleams like a flaming sword throughout the sagas, and they would make dismal reading if the style were not brilliant and the images drawn vivid and picturesque, set as they are in the framework of truth and showing a profound knowledge of human motives.

Snorre lived in the early 13th century, and among his many works, the Saga of the Kings takes a prominent place. The little that has been referred to in this book is but a shadow of the mighty work Snorre left us. Never since the old classic writers has there been an historian to rival him. Thomas Carlyle has said of Snorre that his Saga of the Kings "deserves, were it once well edited, furnished with accurate maps, chronological summaries etc., to be reckoned among the great history-books of the world". If you visit the old St. Mary's Church in Bergen, you will see his statue outside, facing the harbour, a heavy volume under his arm. For we know that he attended Mass in St. Mary's the last time he was in Norway, before setting sail for Iceland.

Let us quote one of the last pages, relating the victory of King Magnus and the death of Eystein Meyla. Eystein's men were called "birchlegs", for they were so poor that they used birch bark to bind about their legs. The name, at first used disdainfully by their enemies, later became a title of honour among themselves.

"The King was in a room, warming himself by the fire, and there were many with him. Men came with the corpse (of Eystein Meyla) and bore it into the room, and the King bade the people come forward and inspect the body. A man was sitting on a bench in the corner: he was a Birchleg but had remained unnoticed, and when he saw and recognised his chieftain's body he sprang up suddenly, rushed out upon the floor and with his battle-axe struck a blow at King Magnus' neck. One of the King's men lunged at him, and the axe struck lower in the shoulder, wounding him deeply. The

Birchleg then raised his axe again and struck at Orm, the King's brother, who was lying on a bench, and the blow was directed at both his legs; but Orm, seeing this intention, drew up his legs, threw them over his head, and the blow fell on the bench, in which the axe stuck fast. By then the weapons in the Birchleg were so numerous that he could scarcely fall to the ground. They saw he had dragged his entrails after him on the floor; and this man's bravery was highly praised".

Here the Saga ends, for the great King Sverre had already had his life-story recorded as he wished it to be passed on to posterity. But although Sverre was a remarkable man — statesman, warrior and orator — he was no poet. In his youth he had been a priest in the Faroe Islands. He was the son of **1177–1202** Sigurd Mouth and after Eystein Meyla's death became chieftain of the Birchlegs. It was his misfortune that he had to use all his sagacity and energy in combating civil war instead of in performing deeds that should live on after his death. He built fortresses in Trondheim and Bergen, traces of which still remain. Even here in Norway where long mountain marches in snow and storm are expected of a man, King Sverre's swift surprise advances are still legendary.

It is hard to leave the sagas, which bring to life men and women of a past age and tell of their joys and sorrows, virtues and misdeeds. The time that followed is fully documented and it is

not long before the true contents are even more
amentable than the dramatic tales of the sagas.
But before we leave the sagas for good, let us give
you a final taste of their style, to show that honour
and integrity were qualities valued above all else.

It is the story of the Icelander Audun and his
polar bear. The anonymous author unfolds his
tale, slowly and in detail, of the impoverished
Audun who with all his wordly possessions bought
a snow-white bear and sailed southwards to present
this wondrous beast to King Svein of Denmark.
On his way he visited Norway, ruled by Harald
Hardrada, who was King Svein's enemy. Harald
wanted to buy the bear from Audun, but the Icelander replied that it was intended for King Svein.
"Well", said King Harald, "but come back and tell
me what Svein gave you for the bear. Who knows?
— you may be fortunate". The narrator continues
his tale, without hurrying to the point, and tells
us of Audun's adventures in Denmark, until finally
he is back again at King Harald's court in Norway.
The King asked him how he had fared. Had his
luck held? What did he get for the bear? Audun
replied: "King Svein thanked me". Harald said
he would have done the same, but what more?
Yes, King Svein had given him money, sufficient
to take him on a pilgrimage to Rome and back.
"King Svein is a pious man", retorted Harald, "he
has helped many a pilgrim to Rome, even those
who had no white bear to give. But was there no
more?" "He honoured me and wanted to make me

his page". "That was well done. Was that all?" "He gave me a ship with a full cargo; no better cargo ever came to Norway". "That was a royal gesture, but I would have done as much". "He gave me a leather bag full of silver coins, so that I should not be poor even if the ship be wrecked". "That was very generous", said Harald, "and I do not think I would have done as much. I would have considered the ship good enough payment. Did you get more?" "Yes, My Lord. King Svein put this golden bracelet on my arm, for he said that a man could lose even money, but the bracelet would be saved if my life be spared. He said I was not to give it away to any man who was not his equal or better. And now I give it to you, King Harald, for you could have *taken* the bear!'

*

1240   The murderous years of Civil War had passed, and King Haakon Haakonssøn held his court in Bergen, the capital at the time. He was a popular king and his reign was long and settled; his fleet was large and well equipped, the people prospered and all was well. He named his son Magnus joint King of the land of Norway with him, and had him crowned on the day he married the Danish princess Ingeborg. To celebrate these events a great banquet was held in the hall now called "Haakons-hallen" which stands at the entrance to the harbour of Bergen. Haakon's fame travelled far and wide; his daughter married a Spanish prince who may not have been to her liking, though the match

brought great honour to the Norwegian royal house. Never has Norway prospered as during the reign of Haakon Haakonssøn. But the old king met his death only two years after the crowning of his son. When the King of Scotland laid claim to the Hebrides and the Isle of Man, Haakon sailed westward to defend his territory, and here he fell ill and died in the Orkneys.

His son, Magnus Lawmender, was a peaceful man *1263–80* who struck a bargain with the King of Scotland regarding these domains, and sold them to him. His fine cognomen was given him for having had our old laws collected to form a common law for the whole kingdom.

Travellers in our country may remark upon the white stone churches with Gothic portals to be found in our valleys or on the headlands in the fjords. When they ask how old the church is, the answer will probably be that it was raised in Magnus Lawmender's time.

At the monastery of St. Olav's in Bergen he erected a church which he intended as a burial place for himself, and although the church is now very much changed, the porch is still a joy to behold.

Magnus was succeeded by his son Eirik, called the Priesthater. His queen was Margaret, daughter **1280–99** of King Alexander of Scotland. She was 20 when she married Eirik, a boy of 12. Queen for only two years, she died giving birth to another little Margaret. This child had a tragic fate, the theme of many a mournful Scottish lay. Her mother's family having died out, the Scots elected the Norwegian princess as their rightful queen and ruler. She sailed from Norway, at the age of 7, but died on the way. "The Maid of Norway" never set foot on Scottish soil.

King Eirik, her father, married as his second wife Isabelle Bruce, the sister of the famous Scottish national hero Robert Bruce. She lived to a ripe old age in Norway, as pious and gentle as her brother was warlike and courageous.

1299–1319 The storm clouds gathered .... In Trondheim

Cathedral are the remains of a sculpture which probably represents King Haakon V. His forehead is puckered with worried lines, and he certainly had good reason for anxiety for the country's economy

46

Akershus

was in a miserable state. German merchants belonging to the powerful Hanseatic League threatened to gain control of his largest town, Bergen. King Haakon removed his court to Oslo, where he built the fortress of Akershus and made it the seat of the government. From that time, Oslo has been the capital of Norway.

After the death of Haakon V, Norway for some years shared a king with Sweden, as his daughter had married a Swedish prince. The Black Death raged with greater violence here than in any **1349** other land. It ravaged the whole of Europe, but no one country suffered more devastation than Norway whose population, small and thinly spread out before, was now reduced by a third. It was reflected in low crops and general poverty, while at the same time the German merchants took the opportunity of loaning money to the needy kings and demanding ever increasing privileges in return.

The Black Death left lasting memories in our folklore. To this day, there are numbers of place names belonging to formerly prosperous farms which were lost and overgrown after the pest, later to be found buried in the heart of forest land. A picturesque tale is told of a hunter who shot an arrow into the air and heard it fall upon resounding metal, which proved to be the bell of an old, overgrown church. There is also the story of the bear who used a deserted church for his winter quarters.

1347 The last successor to the kingdom of Harald Fairhair, Olav, died at the age of 17. Since then, we have had no Olav on the throne of Norway, until our present Olav V succeeded his father, Haakon VII, in 1957.

1380–1412 The country was in a precarious condition, and the nobles, even if they attempted it, were powerless to stem the tide of events. Olav's able mother, the Danish princess Margarete, took over the rule of Denmark, Norway and Sweden. She was a great asset to the throne of Denmark, but of little benefit to us. She added three golden crowns to her coat-of-arms, and the Swedes use this as their national crest to this day. Sweden succeeded in severing this bond, but Denmark and Norway continued to share a king for four centuries. The court was in Copenhagen, and Norway hardly saw the king but only his sheriffs who came to collect taxes.

Of the period which now follows there is little to relate, for we do not know much about these *Dark Years,* as we call them, and the little we know is nothing to rejoice over. We accepted the king elected in Denmark, for we had no choice in the matter. A dynasty of German descent, the Olden-burgers, sat on the Danish throne, and they had troubles of their own and little time or inclination to concern themselves with our difficulties.

The most interesting of these kings was Christian II, a typical Renaissance monarch, violent and **1513–23** ruthless. He lived for five years in Norway, acting as viceroy for his father, and in Bergen he fell in love with the beautiful and gentle Dyveke, daughter of a Dutchwoman who kept a small baker's shop. The prince took mother and daughter back with him to Denmark, the mother as his adviser, the daughter as his devoted mistress. But their life together was dogged by tragedy, for Dyveke died young, probably poisoned, and the King in his despair executed a nobleman suspected of the crime, without waiting for proof. The influence of Sigbrit, the Dutch peasant woman, continued after her daughter's death. After a series of violent events, Sweden also acknowledged Christian as king, but he began his reign with a massacre of his enemies so savage and extreme that one must doubt his sanity. On the day of his coronation, in 1513, his ministers arranged his marriage to a pathetic little princess, Elisabeth, the sister of the German emperor Charles V. She remained by her husband's side in good and evil days, mostly the latter, and followed him into exile. In Europe she sought out her high-born relations to beg help for her ex-king husband. But she too died young and was thus spared his deepest humiliation.

Christian managed to equip a fleet with which he set sail for Norway where he believed he would find supporters. In Oslo he was decoyed on board a ship where the emissaries of the new Danish King had agreed to parley with him and had pledged their word that no harm should come to him. But they held him prisoner and took him to Denmark, where he remained imprisoned for 17 long years. According to legend, he wore a groove in the table in his cell, as he strode restlessly round and round, his hand pressing on the table top.

Norway reached the lowest depths of humiliation in 1536, when the Parliament in Copenhagen elected Christian III as king, accepted the Lutheran reformed church and proclaimed Norway henceforth as part of Denmark, no longer a separate kingdom. Not one man in the land of Norway had the power or authority to protest effectively.

The Catholic clergy had long been the only power in Norway that could stand up against the autocratic officials sent by the Danish kings. When the clergy were expelled, our country, in common with other countries under the Reformation, resounded to the crash of falling masonry as convents and monasteries were demolished and despoiled. But as to the resolution that Norway should cease to be a separate country, the vanity of the King unexpectedly came to our aid. It is, of course, a more impressive title to be King of Denmark and Norway. And that little conjunction "and" later became a straw to which Norwegians clung when we

The ruins of Hamar Cathedral.

were close to drowning. But we are coming to that!

From now on, Norway slowly recovered her strength. Only a faint echo reached us here of the Renaissance which in other countries was a glorious rebirth and a time of great achievement. We were struggling for our very existence and this demanded all our efforts.

In the year of 1624, Oslo suffered a great fire, and Christian IV had the ruins razed to the ground and built the city up again, for its greater protection, under the walls of Akershus fortress. He called the town Christiania after himself, and the capital kept this name for exactly 300 years, until in 1924 it was decided to revert to the old name of Oslo.

Christian IV was a good king for Norway, for he **1588–1648** concerned himself with the affairs of his northerly domain, and his initials C4 are seen over many a beautiful portal and on fittings in churches to this day.

While Christian IV was ruling in Denmark and Norway, his sister Anne became betrothed to the young King James of Scotland, and her Royal Highness sailed from Copenhagen with a fine fleet headed for Edinburgh. Heavy storms drove her ships off their course and swept them northwards to Oslo, where she landed seasick and forlorn. Here she was given the best quarters available, though they were not exactly princely. James, her bridegroom, **1589** was no hero, nor was he noted for his impulsive actions, but for once in his life he acted quickly and decisively. He crossed the stormy North Sea and landed at Oslo, where a simple marriage ceremony took place in a house of which part still survives. For lack of other dowry for his sister, Christian IV mortgaged the Orkney Islands to the Scottish king, and they were never redeemed. The Shetlands had already suffered the same fate under his ancestor Christian I.

King Christian IV saw his sister again when she was Queen of England. To commemorate this visit,

Shakespeare borrowed a Danish theme for one of his plays, "Hamlet", and he certainly made the most of his subject.

The joint kingdoms of Denmark and Norway were seldom fortunate in war, but on a few occasions luck was with them. Christian IV coveted the laurels of a warrior king, and so did the King of Sweden. War was inevitable, but though Sweden was defeated the result made no alteration in the prevailing position. This is an event in our history which we recall with pride, for the King of Sweden was the young Gustaf Adolf, the hero of the Thirty Years' War and later famous for his victories.

While our war with Sweden was raging, the Swedish leaders hired a detachment of mercenaries from Scotland, under the command of Col. Ramsay. Three hundred men went ashore at Romsdal in Norway, where they calculated that their landing would be least expected. The daring plan was to cross the mountains in forced marches and reach the Swedish border though the Gudbrand Valley. Local tradition tells a dire tale of their ravages on their way, but history gives the lie to these stories. They were in too much of a hurry to get to their destination and crossed the mountains with all possible speed, yet rumour preceded them. Folk tradition extols the outstanding courage of the peasants in attacking these professional soldiers, whereas historians stress the quick reaction of the local population. They gathered in the mountains at Kringen, armed with axes and great stones, and massacred the Scots to a man. One of the Scottish junior officers, George Sinclair, has gone down to history as the hero of this episode, while the name of Ramsay has been forgotten. On many a farmhouse wall in the Gudbrand Valley hangs a rusty sword which is proudly pointed out as a Scottish trophy, and some families claim to be the descendants of the only Scot who escaped at Kringen. But the sad truth is that not one was spared, for the peasants acted as men do when fear, their first motive, changes into the intoxication of victory.

Mention has already been made of the Hanseatic merchants, a strong contingent of whom had ensconced themselves in Bergen, then the largest town in Norway. The course of events here is interesting, and I shall try to describe its development.

When people settled on the coast in the olden days, the first houses to be built were the sheds by the quay; everything else was of minor importance and came by degrees. In Bergen we are in the unique position of being able to follow the growth and development of the town from its earliest days, in the remains now being excavated on the site of the fire of 1955, when the 18th century copies of earlier houses burned to the ground.

Around the year 1075 there was a royal residence at Holmen, the headland jutting out into the fjord at the approach to Bergen harbour, and a road led from the farms in the bay along the coast to this estate. Between the road and the harbour were rows of wharfs with sheds where the farmers sheltered their boats and the travelling pedlars offered their wares for sale. King Olav Kyrre raised a church on this site, near the harbour, and gave the town many rights and privileges, whereby more and more people were attracted to the growing township. Rows of wooden buildings now stretched up from the sea, the alleys between just wide enough for two people to pass. Down by the wharfs the boats were anchored, up by the road were the merchants' booths and the taverns. These clusters of timber dwellings were extremely inflammable, and therefore it was the custom to have all food cooked in specially constructed buildings, usually of stone, which stood a little apart. Those who lived in these rows of warehouses ate in these communal kitchens, and the arrangement was that all of them paid their share of the expenses into a common pool — or "Schøt".

The lively trade in Bergen came under German control when the kings sold the monopoly for cash and Norwegians were ousted from their old trading centre. They were obliged to build houses elsewhere in the town, on the other side of the inner harbour. On the "German Quay" the Hanseats kept the old style of building, and if the wooden buildings burned down they built them up again on the same architectural principles; but the wharf itself was usually moved some yards further out into the harbour to give room for ships which required deeper anchorage. The merchants' houses retained their old Norse names (Engelgaarden, Finnegaarden, Bugaarden), and their insignia were painted wooden figure-heads over the doors or entrance to each narrow alley between the long rows of buildings. But life within these walls was very different under the Hanseats, for their League had stern laws, one of which was strict celibacy. They kept the custom of communal meals, a convenient arrangement for bachelors, and maintained rigid discipline, based largely on punishment by flogging. But they also had their lighter moments, when beer flowed like water.

The Hanseatic merchants adopted King Eystein's ancient Church of St. Mary's as their parish church, and put up epitaphs to deceased League members with inscriptions in German. It is interesting to note that services in German were held in St. Mary's as late as 1868.

But the might of the Hanseatic League gradually crumbled, and towards the end of the 16th century their power in Bergen was dealt a decisive blow. In this connection we remember with gratitude the names of two successive Danish governors at Bergen Fortress (Bergenhus): Walckendorff and Rosenkrantz. They summoned Scottish masons to assist in the building of the great tower now known as the Rosenkrantz Tower, designed to protect Bergen not only against enemies from without but also against the Germans on the Quay, under the very walls of the tower. It was a very impressive fortress, and among its prisoners it can count the

famous James Hepburn, Earl of Bothwell, who was forced to flee from Scotland a week after his marriage to Mary, Queen of Scots, and later was imprisoned here.

The Hanseatic League was finally dissolved in 1630, and a number of German merchants settled in Bergen, married and had families. Many Norwegian surnames today bear witness to German origin. The German Quay was no longer used as a residential quarter, but as warehouses and offices only. Fires were rife in these timber buildings, soaked in cod-liver oil and piled high with hay and fodder, and those which have survived were

rebuilt after the great fire in 1702. Foreigners no doubt wonder a little why we value so highly the few houses that remain. The explanation is that we value them because to the historically-minded observer they represent continuity stretching unbroken over nine centuries of turbulent life — where the unimaginative can see only rotting woodwork.

On the burned-out sites of the fire of 1955, under the remains of walls and piles and quays, are nowadays found thousands of interesting objects, in themselves of no value: broken pottery, worn shoes, knife sheaths, pieces of wood inscribed with runic characters and all kinds of relics which tell us more graphically than any written records how people lived in those days. The remarkable thing is that on this busy spot, with its teeming life, the medieval architecture and "street planning" has survived through the centuries.

Walckendorff and Rosenkrantz, these two Danish governors of Bergen, have left lasting memorials, Walckendorff's residence has ever since served as the Town Hall. It was restored and enlarged in in the 18th century, but it is, nevertheless, the original home of Walckendorff. Rosenkrantz built his private house as an arch straddling the old Strandgaten, and here it still stands — a picturesque feature of the city of Bergen.

Norway, too, had its share of great men. There *1690–1720* was, for instance, the intrepid Peter Wessel from Trondheim, who was made admiral and knighted under the name of Tordenskjold ("Thunder Shield"). He possessed all the qualities, which betoken the true officer — foresightedness, thoroughness in planning, resourcefulness in action. The few letters he wrote have their place in our national literature on account of their simple, straightforward style, and that is no light praise for a man living in the sophisticated 18th century.

The man he was called upon to fight was King Karl XII of Sweden, one of history's great generals, a brilliant man, and yet of such austerity that no poor churl lived more sparingly than he. He grudged himself both food and sleep, and no one in the entire Kingdom of Sweden was hardier and braver than the King himself, a man sans women, sans wine and song — even sans the fashionable peri-

wig of his time. He was proof against all temptation, except the desire for military honour and glory, and this lust — for lust it was — led to disaster, both for himself and for his country. After many a brilliant victory and strategic triumph he died, at the age of 36, leaving his country, formerly a strong nation, weakened by his many campaigns. This military genius, feared throughout Europe, was our respected enemy in Tordenskjold's day. According to Voltaire who was the first to write a biography of Karl XII, when the Great Powers signed a pact to defeat him, he followed the tactics of Hannibal: unable to defend his own country, he launched an attack on the country of his enemy. With his famous regiments, in their well known blue and yellow uniforms, Karl XII marched into Norway and laid siege to the fortress of Akershus in Oslo (Christiania). Even now, centuries after his death, the name of Karl XII inspires feelings of respect for his great talents — and horror over the use he made of them. In 1718 King Karl laid siege to Fredriksten Fort at Halden in south-east Norway: his men were digging themselves in, and while the King himself stood in a trench, looking towards the fort, a bullet hit him full in the temple and killed him on the spot. No doubt he was hit by a chance bullet from the fort, but the thought cannot readily be dismissed that one of his own men may have wished to rid his country of their militarist king who brought such disaster to his land.

Our naval hero Tordenskjold fought successfully against this worthy opponent, his greatest victory being the battle of Dynekilen, when he destroyed King Karl's transports. **1716**

When foreign naval ships today anchor up in Oslo harbour, the first Norwegian to greet them is Tordenskjold, on his pedestal. A memorial also stands at the spot where Karl XII fell at Halden, and it is whispered that his ghost walks here. But this rumour is not sufficiently well founded to be included among the tourist attractions of Norway.

Another of Norway's illustrious sons is Ludvig Holberg the dramatist, born in Bergen, who settled in Copenhagen and became a professor and a baron. He combined two qualities rarely seen together: he was both a careful economist and a spirited writer. His comedies are simple and merry, **1684–1754** and have gained him the name of the Molière of the North. He is also known as the father of Danish dramatic art, and this makes him all the more dear to us who claim him as a Norwegian. He himself recognised no difference between the two nations, for both owed homage to the same king. Holberg's comedies are still performed regularly in our theatres.

The years rolled by, and Europe was shaken by the French Revolution and all it brought in its wake — Napoleon and his ill-fated military ambition. But here in the North the peasants and fishermen lived out their quiet, austere lives as their forefathers had done before them. In our country, with its long coast-line, its great forests, high mountain plateaux and deep fjords, a folk culture slowly developed, characteristic of each separate district, neither rich nor splendid, it is true, but with a charm and appeal all its own.

The influence from abroad was most strongly noticeable in the south of Norway and in Bergen. People lived in white-painted houses which reflected the classic ideal, then fashionable in France, but with its cold marble replaced by the warmer material wood, for the use of the bourgeois Norwegian in a colder climate. We can still see this architectural style in the coastal towns which have escaped the big fires — Mandal and Lillesand, for instance — townships which bear witness to the days when Norwegian windjammers sailed the seven seas and their crew returned with strange souvenirs from many lands — great conch shells, pictures of Vesuvius in eruption and suchlike exotic homecoming gifts.

The Town Hall and Customs House in these old towns frequently bear the monogram of C7 on the gables. This stands for Christian VII, a sadly deranged little man married to the lively English princess Caroline Mathilde, sister of George III. She was only 15 when she was crowned Queen of Denmark and Norway, and just six years later an English emissary took her away from Kronborg Castle, divorced and cast aside. Neither she nor her husband ever saw their kingdom of Norway. **1772**

Now at last, a period of prosperity and progress dawned for Norway. By the rushing rivers sawmills were built, and the timber industry was established. In the larger ports shipyards were founded, and agriculture flourished in the broad valleys and meadows, particularly of the more fertile east country. As a consequence of greater prosperity, a more gracious way of living developed, and this was reflected in the many beautiful manor-houses built at the end of the 18th century. They are by no means castles, but pleasant backgrounds for the lives of cultured hard-working men. From this period date our most gracious residences, designed as a rule by the clergyman or officer who

was to be its occupant. It was the heyday of the gifted amateur of the arts.

The further away from the towns, the more strongly individual became the local style, each valley having its own characteristics. Here, the houses are built of logs, almost black with age. The roofs were covered with turf upon which flowers grew. The oldest of these rural houses had only a hole in the roof through which the smoke escaped from the fire on the floor beneath. The bedcovers were pelts, and food was served in wooden bowls and eaten with wooden spoons. There was poverty, even dire poverty, but the fish in the lakes and streams and the reindeer roaming the mountains and forests were everyman's property, and although a small farm in the west country could feed as many as worked upon it, it demanded hard and continuous labour. These farmers had no easy task, it is true, but at least they did not wear themselves out for a master they never saw, who lived at court and sent officials to collect his dues for him. These simple men had a fearless independence of word and deed which proved to be of greater use than wealth when our country was suddenly and unexpectedly put to the test.

Our most important open air museums, the Norwegian Folk Museum at Bygdøy, Oslo, and the Sandvig Collection at Lillehammer, are both rich sources of information for anybody wishing to study our peasant culture. Fine old farm-houses have been moved here bodily, with all their contents, and provide us with a living picture-book of cultural history. But what particularly gladdens our hearts in this connection is that nothing of what we find in these outdoor museums is so obsolete that we cannot also find it in full use to this very day in the country districts. Medieval log houses can still be found in various places by those who know were to look. Some of our finest stave churches are still in use in remote valleys, and the curious erections simply called "lofts" still stand among ordinary farm buildings and betray their medieval origin in every line. Let us examine these lofts at close quarters:

In olden days, no other method of heating was known except the open hearth on the floor, from

Finneloftet at Voss was built more than
700 years ago.

whence the smoke rose through a hole in the roof. In very remote valleys, houses were built after this style until well into the last century.

The next step was to move the hearth into a corner, but the smoke still had to find its way out through the roof of the windowless house. In the 18th century, iron stoves for the burning of logs made their appearance, and made it possible to build two-storey houses with a stove in each room.

The danger of fire was naturally much greater in those days when, before matches were invented, fire had to be kept alight night and day. This is the reason it was so difficult to warm houses in the Middle Ages, and in many cases impossible. Two-storey dwelling houses could not be warmed, especially if they were built on piles, as many were in Norway. These were called "stabbur" and were used as storehouses, which explains the pile construction to keep rats and mice away. On larger farms it was the custom to build a particularly spacious, airy room — a "loft" — over the storeroom, and this was where the young girls lived. Here the family kept their most precious belongings of silver and cloth, and it was here they retreated in the event of attack. But not all storerooms had lofts, and not all lofts are built over store-rooms. The loft could sometimes be used for weddings and other feasts, or it could have the character of a private parlour where the women of the household could retire with their handwork or the family heads confer. The common characteristic of these "lofts" is that they could not be heated by an open hearth fire, and this is probably the reason why so many have been preserved to this day.

We Norwegians always visualize our national heroes against a background of blackened log walls, for the houses were very similar in design, only varying in size, for peasant and patrician. A paved threshold led to a massive iron-studded door, nearly as broad as it was long, and narrow, steep stairways formed the approach to the women's quarters. Norwegian literature must be read into this same background when it has an old peasant setting, as in Ibsen's "Peer Gynt" and in Sigrid Undset's famous medieval novel "Kristin Lavransdatter".

Northwards up the coast, the folk relics in our country museums are very sparse and poor, and we feel intense sympathy with the struggling population that has left behind little but the tools of its trade, fish-hooks, nets, seagoing garments of skin, traps to catch wild animals. One sees in imagination a flock of hungry men, ever on the look-out for food in the forests and the mountain rivers. Their boat was their most faithful companion. For centuries our forefathers have sailed the seas to cast their nets and to find markets for their fish, but the courage and seamanship of these men cannot be exhibited in a museum.

Far, far to the north, the Lapps live their nomadic lives as they have always done throughout the centuries. Little development can be traced, for they have long since learned all they needed for their way of life, and in spite of modern inventions, life on the great mountain plateaux remains the same as it has always been.

Scattered over the whole length of Norway are white churches and houses raised by the officials of the Crown at the turn of the 18th century. But none of these remain in Finnmark, in the far north, for here every single house and cottage was burned to the ground during the last war. In the Lapp village of Karasjok only the church, built in 1800, remains intact, all else is now newly built. This very church, so touching in its classic simpli-

city, faintly reminiscent of the marble columns of
the distant Acropolis, was the spiritual home of a
lonely priest who drove his reindeer sleigh over the
snowy wastes of Finnmark to visit his parishioners.

This is how life in Norway was lived in the days
when Napoleon harassed the regents of Europe
into early graves. Napoleon's armies stood in readi-
ness at the border of Denmark, and King Frederik
VI was forced to promise his friendship and support. This, naturally, brought him into conflict
with England, with whom the twin kingdoms of
Denmark and Norway had never had any serious
disagreement before. Frederik had a fine fleet
which Napoleon was planning to use in his invasion of England, and to hinder the execution of
this scheme, Nelson crossed the North Sea and put
the fleet out of action at the battle of Copenhagen, **1801**
although at that time Denmark and Norway were
not at war with England. In this way our country

was drawn into the European conflict on the side with which we felt least sympathy, and we were obliged to pay our share of Napoleon's war debts. Frederik VI was forced to sign a peace treaty, on the 14th January, 1814, by which he handed Norway over to Sweden.

The news of this aroused wrath and despair in Norway, and her leading men declared that the King had no right to hand over a kingdom which was not his to dispose of. The ideas of the French Revolution had found an echo in the hearts of Norwegians, while a growing interest in history reminded us that we had at one time elected the King of Denmark to be our king; he ruled by our own request, not by force of conquest.

In four short months a council of the country's leading men was called together, a summons was sent out for the election of representatives to a parliament, elections were held, the chosen members met and held conferences to lay the foundation of a constitution, and finally they all swore an oath of allegiance. This feat bears witness to resolute courage and a spirit which arouses our national pride and admiration. Let it be remembered that our country at that time had very poor roads and no other means of communication; we were isolated from the outside world and at war with our neighbour Sweden. In addition, we had had no form of self-government before, nor for centuries any leaders elected by the people. The King of both kingdoms was absolute, at least nominally; his

officials were chosen in Copenhagen and managed the affairs of our country according to their own ideas. It was, in those days, a century and a half ago, a fantastic achievement to muster such a gathering of national spokesmen, even though we could not summon representatives from the districts farthest north, from Nordland, Troms and Finn-mark.

They came from all quarters, these earnest men — on horseback, by boat, by road and on foot. Their destination was Eidsvoll, a day's journey from Christiania. The assembly was held in the manor-house at Eidsvoll Verk, the property of a rich patriot who placed it at the disposal of the new parliament. The place was not casually chosen, for Eidsvoll had been the seat of gatherings called "things" in days gone-by, and the name was associated with the Sagas in the minds of all Norwegians. Among the 112 men who met together at Eidsvoll there were clergymen, officers, lawyers and landowners, a few rich merchants and a single solitary count. They were fortunate in that two of their number, Wilhelm Christie and Christian

Magnus Falsen, both of them lawyers, stood out as obvious leaders. Both were young men, 36 and 32 respectively.

The idea of self-government was in the air; the form a constitution should take had been discussed among able men on previous occasions, and the men at Eidsvoll had a clear picture of the type of government that was required for their country.

With Falsen as leader and Christie as secretary the work was accomplished with all possible speed. It had to be, for the Swedish army was on the march from France and the Norwegians knew that it was essential to have their demands defined at the exacting and difficult parleys ahead of them. Although they did not reach complete agreement on all points, a draft of the constitution was finally drawn up, the representatives joined hands and swore faithful allegiance to the constitution "so long as the mountains of Norway stand". This memorable day, the 17th of May, has since been celebrated as our National Day, our Day of Independence.

They placed the power of election in the hands of the farmers, believing that the free smallholder is the man who has best reason to defend his property and his rights. The leading men of the Constituent Assembly, being university men and civil servants, knew from experience that the peasant population had little learning and still less practice than themselves in government administration, yet they placed the electoral power in their hands. No doubt they trusted the peasants to choose their representatives from among the ranks of officials, in gratitude for the confidence placed in their judgement. Nevertheless, their faith in the common people was remarkable.

Norwegian children are, naturally, taught the history of the men of Eidsvoll in a simplified version. We were told that they were brave, wise, upright and farsighted. But in this sceptical age one has tried to find in these men traces of ignorance and egotism where before the idealists saw only love of freedom and proud independence. We are unconvinced: from any point of view what happened in 1814 was a marvellous achievement. The constitution these men drew up was, according to the standards of the day, amazingly democratic, bordering even on the radical. Not much remains today of its original form, for one of its best qualities was the flexibility that allowed for natural development. Norwegians have, on the whole, been satisfied with their constitution these past 150 years, and we accord the men of Eidsvoll the honour they deserve.

The Danish prince Christian Frederik was elected king, and after a few skirmishes negotiations were begun with the Swedes, whose leader was their crown prince, Karl Johan, an adversary not to be trifled with.

Christie was spokesman at these negotiations, and it was he who gave the reply which characterised the man himself and the situation. Asked by the

Swedish representatives what the Norwegians had to fall back upon if the negotiations failed, Christie answered in one word: "Desperation!".

It is one thing for a small nation to stand firm and demand its rights but quite another matter whether those in power acknowledge the justice of such claims. If Karl Johan had been the descendant of an ancient royal dynasty, Europe would probably have ignored our demands, however strong our protests. But Karl Johan, the name he assumed, had been Field Marshal Bernadotte in the victorious French army; he had helped Napoleon to become Emperor, and even if later he had assisted in Bonaparte's downfall, he was not anxious for reactionary kings and ministers to interfere in his affairs. As a man of action, he was all for a quick decision. It was obvious that Norway, impoverished and without leaders, would benefit from some form of an alliance with Sweden, and the negotiations resulted in our recognition of the Swedish king as our sovereign, pledged to uphold the new Norwegian constitution.

Wilhelm Christie, that gifted and remarkable man, was by profession a civil servant, and returned to his post in Bergen after these stirring events, having no ambition to seek further national honours. His outline for the constitution was sound and judicious, and he brought delicate negotiations to a successful conclusion. At the age of 36, he had been elected the first president of our Storting — the Father of the Nation — a post he held for six years. In gratitude for his services his fellow members of Parliamant presented him with a gold cup; the King bestowed orders upon him and offered him a seat in his Cabinet, which Christie declined. His health had suffered from the strain of the fateful year of 1814, and he later applied for a comparatively modest post in the Customs Service in Bergen. In his later years he worked tirelessly for the foundation of a museum in his  home town, and Bergen Museum opened its doors in 1825, the first in the land. In front of this building stands Wilhelm Christie, in bronze, the Constitution of Norway in his hand. It may not be a very good statue, but it was the first ever raised in Norway; not even kings of the realm had been accorded such an honour. He was venerated by his contemporaries and by posterity, and the title of president was attached to his name all his life, for he had had the unique honour of being president of our first Parliament. Never has there been a more modest politician; he was not a man to boast of his orders and decorations, and only on one occasion did he draw up a list of them — to gladden the heart of his ageing father.

Christian Magnus Falsen, who has gone down to history as the Father of the Constitution, devoted himself, tirelessly to the cause of his country. He was a man of great courage and willpower: not only was his coiffure reminiscent of the great leaders of the French Revolution, but also the mind beneath it. His exposed position in the service of his country made him unpopular, and petty misunderstandings undermined his health. He was president of the Supreme Court of Justice where he died in 1830, at the age of 47.

These were our two leaders in 1814, and ranged behind them stood men of the same mould. Their adversary, Karl Johan, was a man of a different stamp: Bernadotte, to give him his original name, had been a professional soldier before the French Revolution, and had risen rapidly from the ranks. Desirée, Napoleon's first love, became his wife and, in 1804, he was promoted to be Marshal of France and Prince of Ponte Corvo. In 1809, no longer on good terms with the Emperor, he resigned from the French Army. At that time Sweden was without an heir apparent; war was raging on all sides and it was important that the country should have a military leader. The choice fell on Bernadotte, a man whom his army would follow and the citizens could admire. He came to Sweden, took the name of Karl Johan and led the Swedish army against France, afterwards sharing the spoils of victory.

After the fall of Napoleon, Bernadotte did not feel too secure on the throne of Sweden, for reaction set in throughout Europe. Old reckonings were brought up — and who was this Karl Johan?

A common private who had taken part in the Revolution and fought in Napoleon's army. It was essential for him to settle his affairs quietly and expeditiously before the Great Powers decided to do it for him. He agreed to uphold our constitution, with the few changes required as a result of a union with Sweden, but he was not pleased. What kind of a country was this? No castle to live in, no nobility, no court to surround him; few even understood his language. Nevertheless, he became a good king for Norway. His personal charm won him friends even among those who disliked his politics. His large private fortune enabled him to act generously, and his career was an adventure in itself. Our greatgrandfathers had a saying when they wanted to impress upon their children the virtue of patience: "If you wait patiently, you may become King of Sweden!" Karl Johan came to the throne in 1818; he bestrides his bronze horse outside the Royal Palace in Oslo, or Christiania, as it was called right up to 1924, which was built during his reign.

It is difficult to leave the period which includes the historic date of 1814, the most fascinating epoch in our history. It is gratifying to record that these simple patriots should have achieved the aim they had set themselves, to lay the foundation for their country's growth and progress. They had so little to build upon: experience, economic security and skilled professional men were lacking. A country parson made the first chronometer for our young university, founded in 1811, another cleric became professor of marine zoology. It was an officer, not an architect, who designed the King's palace, the owner of an ironwork who translated Snorre's famous sagas from Old Norse into Danish, the official language at the time.

Travellers to Norway in those days found little to write home about. Nobody had yet discovered the beauty and characteristic charm of the mountains and fjords of Norway. Those who lived among them were perhaps aware of it, and poets had written about our "proud" peaks, but not of their beauty. Neither had the Norwegian landscape been immortalised in paint. Most people, and certainly most educated townfolk, considered that the higher a mountain, the uglier it was. A cultural milieu, where artistic life could thrive, did not exist. True enough, the educated upper classes practised music, drawing, play-acting, the latter even in

French, but we had no professional artists. The only fine building from olden times worthy of holding a place in European architecture was the Nidaros Cathedral at Trondheim, at that time practically in ruins.

But come they did, the men we needed for our future growth as a nation, not by a sudden miracle but through long years of labour and toil. The first was the painter I. C. Dahl, a poor apprentice who showed such artistic talent that philanthropists paid for his art training in Germany. Dahl justified his faith and later became a respected professor at the Academy in Dresden. He spent his summers in Norway, making hundreds of sketches; he rode on his agile mountain pony right up to the snow limit and everywhere he went he made drawings, beautiful little studies of our mountain peaks and broad valleys — while his horse grazed peacefully and the local guide watched him in wonderment. Back in Germany for the winter, he painted the splendid landscapes which today hang in our art galleries, the first pictures to show the world the beauty of Norwegian mountains.

Ole Bull was our first violinist of international fame. Handsome, charming and successful, he has left a legend behind him which is alive to this day, first and foremost on account of his fame as a violinist, but also because he was a staunch patriot and declared that the natural scenery of his native land, the folklore and sagas told to him in childhood had inspired his work. He was a true romantic, and this trend in him, which never faded, has created an atmosphere of magic around his name. Ole Bull is the founder of the Bergen theatre.

Our fairy tales and folklore, sagas and lays, deserve a chapter to themselves. In the winter evenings, when all was quiet around the fire and only the hum of the spinning-wheel would be heard, was the time for the story-teller to unfold his tale and for old songs to be sung. But now townsfolk began to interest themselves in these things and ask for them to be collected and recorded by experts. This is how our folk-tales came to be printed. They were collected by P. Chr.

Asbjørnsen, a zoologist and forester by profession, and by the country parson, later a bishop, Jørgen Moe. The lively prose and strange fantasies of these tales made them popular, and later, when they were illustrated by the artists Erik Werenskiold and Theodor Kittelsen, they became even more prized. These two artists not only succeeded in bringing to life creatures which had existed only in the national imagination, but they did so in such a way that all Norwegians feel an instinctive kinship with them; trolls and other weird beings are, in fact, part and parcel of the national heritage.

Unfortunately, these trolls have begotten many sadly degenerate offspring in our days, in souvenir shops: a multitude of monsters, small and large, carved in wood and hung about with moss, with red noses and patched trousers. Few of these are genuine trolls; most of them are of miserably poor stock and bear little relation to the royal giants who lived in our mountains in days gone by.

Landstad, another pioneer, was parish priest of a small medieval stone church with narrow windows and a little spire, which stood between forest-clad slopes and blue lakes in the country of Telemark. To reach all his parishioners he had to ride far afield. In gratitude for the spiritual comfort he brought them, his people sang old lays for him, about bold knights who risked their lives for the sake of beautiful maidens, who fought dragons or avenged their fathers. They sang about the dead who spoke from their graves, and of the rose-tree which grew from the tomb of ill-fated lowers, of men who could see beyond death and predict Doomsday.

Landstad's collection of folk-songs when published revealed a new world of folklore. The primitive beauty of these tunes is like the sight of alpine flowers on stony ground, and makes an immediate appeal to all who appreciate simplicity.

Lindemann gave our church a hymnal where he had collected popular hymns, set to melodies composed by simple and devoted men, whose names are lost to posterity. They proved beyond doubt that artistic talent existed whenever the opportunities for expression presented themselves.

This is how Norwegians in the last century set about exploring their own country, and these are the treasures they found. And as time went by we were fortunate enough to breed the men we needed, each in his own field.

The Constitution gave us a Parliament — "Storting" we call it — but we had no building in which to house it until 1866. Nevertheless, it was a true parliament, even though the members sat on narrow benches in an improvised hall. Most of the men of Eidsvoll in 1814 had been officials and civil servants, but, as we have seen, they placed the electoral power in the hands of the peasant population. It was not without a certain amount of conflict that the farmers and smallholders, in the course of time, secured the right to elect the members of the Storting from their own ranks.

As we know, mountains of paper are required to build up a state, and our statesmen have been no exception in this respect, as the task of law-making has proceeded on its way.

Two great tasks faced our first Storting: to secure the internal economy of the country and to uphold our constitution in our freely accepted union with Sweden. It was not necessary to be concerned with foreign policy, for that we shared with Sweden. 1884 is the year when we reckon that parliamentary government, in the modern sense of the term, came into being here, under the leadership of Johan Sverdrup, who is regarded as the most gifted politician in our history. There were only two political parties in those days, "Right" and "Left", and the peasant population felt most at home with the latter party, led by Sverdrup. His aim was clearly defined in the statement: "All power shall be concentrated in this assembly".

Relations with the Swedish King of the Union were not always of the best, for the Norwegians tried to annul one by one the paragraphs in the Union Agreement which tended to make us subservient to Sweden. The King and his Swedish ministers naturally wished the twin kingdoms to appear to the outside world united and of one mind. According to the terms of the Constitution the royal veto could be invoked twice against any act passed by the Storting; a third passage of a bill, however, made it law, regardless of the King's wishes.

One source of friction was the question of our flag. We had no flag of our own before 1814, when we used the red Danish flag with the white cross, with the addition of a lion with an axe in the top corner. A Norwegian flag, with a blue cross inside the white Danish one, was voted by the Storting. The struggle over this flag lasted as long as our union with Sweden, and is as obscure as it is boring to follow. The Swedish blue-and-yellow flag was combined with the Norwegian red-white-and-blue in a peculiarly hideous combination, popularly known as "herring salad". A continual quarrel went on as to when the Swedish flag should be used, when the Swedish flag with the Union emblem in the top corner, when the Norwegian flag with the emblem — or whether an unquartered "Norwegian" flag could be permitted at all, and if so, when. Our naval ensign, which was to represent us in foreign ports, bore the Union emblem right up to the dissolution of the Union in 1905. The contest was a vigorous one, energetically debated both at the King's table and round the family dinner table. Here is an anecdote, a true one, which bears witness to the humour and resource of the leading men of the day:

Christian Michelsen, a rich shipowner in Bergen, was a radical, a man fearless in the Battle of the Flag as in other conflicts. From his flagstaff he never flew any other flag but the unquartered Norwegian flag, without the Union emblem. One day the King came to Bergen on his travels and was invited to visit Michelsen, then Mayor of Bergen, at his home. King Oscar II was a regal figure, and no one could tell from his aspect that inwardly he was bothered by the crucial question: "What flag will the Mayor fly?" Michelsen could not lose face with his own followers by flying the hated Union flag, and yet on the other hand he could not insult the King by using a forbidden flag. The whole town was buzzing with excitement and curiosity. As the King drove up, he asked his companion in the carriage: "What flag is flying?" The answer was hesitant, the informer was not sure, but at least it was *not* the Norwegian flag. "I am deeply relieved", said King Oscar. Michelsen had chosen to hoist the civic flag of Bergen!

The Storting became so fiercely national that on occasion they impeached the King's ministers if they supported the King in his opposition to resolutions of the Storting.

War was one difficulty with which our Storting did not have to contend. During the Napoleonic wars Norwegians too had to get into uniform; no nation seemed to be exempt. They wore the white buckskin breeches, jack-boots, tall shakos and double-breasted jackets that the fashion of the time decreed. Becoming and picturesque, certainly, but impractical, and not even warm.

We regard these soldiers of 1814 as a symbol of heroic patriotism, for they spared their descendants the horrors of war. It is worth recording that

already then the Norwegians had their own ski-companies, at a time when skis were unknown in more southerly lands.

In the years to come, the courage of Norwegians was put to good purpose in other fields than that of battle. Our countrymen dedicated themselves to the sea, and during the following century Norway became one of the leading seafaring nations of the world. Svend Foyn from Tønsberg changed whaling from a hazardous game to a modern industry, by constructing his own vessels, specially designed for the purpose and equipped with harpoon guns.

Norwegian currency notes are all decorated with portraits of men, and a traveller to our country may wish to know something about the men depicted. Who are these leading citizens entrusted with the honour of representing their country? Abel whose head is portrayed on our 500-kroner notes, was one of the gifted young men Norway produced after 1814; he was recognised as a mathematical genius before his untimely death at the age of 26. In front of the palace in

ABEL

Oslo you will see his statue, a man on a tall column, triumphantly erect upon the backs of his geniuses. The sculptor, Vigeland, intended to portray the flight of genius, borne aloft by will-power and intellect, and the statue group represents the nation's homage to Abel.

On three of our notes are the heads of writers: Wergeland, on the red 100-kroner notes, was our first poet of importance after 1814, that vital date to which we inevitably return. He lamented his fate in having been born into a small nation whose language is confined to its own country. He was generous, impulsive, creative and incredibly prolific. There are not many who read his poems today, but those who do acclaim him as wholeheartedly as the Scots their Robert Burns, of whose works he was the translator.

The noble features of Bjørnstjerne Bjørnson are portrayed in green on our 50-kroner notes. He was an active politician, and he and Wergeland were much of the same calibre. But whereas Wergeland died before his 40th year, Bjørnson lived twice as long, and he devoted his life to the many causes, political and social, that interested him. It was he who wrote the text of our national anthem with the opening lines "Norway thine is our devotion/Land of hearth and home/Rising storm-carred from the ocean Were the breakers foam."

The third of the portraits is the most famous of them all, Henrik Ibsen the dramatist, shown on the 1000-kroner notes. You are perhaps familiar with his appearance already, for his fame is world-wide, and his stern old face with its severe mouth and mutton-chop whiskers is known wherever his dramas are played, from Tokio to Hollywood. His plays deal with all aspects of human life and are masterly in their construction. His psychological insight and brilliant technique place him among the greatest names in world literature, and although his works contain many a well-aimed and bitter attack on his own countrymen, yet we take great pride in his fame.

Ibsen's great knowledge was acquired from unknown sources, for his education was meagre. He came from a poor and joyless home, and had great difficulty in making friends. He was appointed director of our first theatre, founded in Bergen in 1850 by Ole Bull, the violinist. It was here, in difficult circumstances, that he learned his trade. The original building, of classic proportions but devoid of all amenities, was destroyed in the Second World War; on this simple, even primitive stage some of Ibsen's plays were performed for the first time, the actors instructed in their parts by Ibsen himself.

These were important years for dramatic art in Norway, and gifted actors played the leading parts in "Peer Gynt", «The Wild Duck» and «A Doll's House". The National Theatre in Oslo was opened at the turn of the century; a new theatre was built in Bergen in 1909, and Ibsen's plays have always provided our actors with their greatest challenge. This new burst of talent in the Norwegian theatre was symbolized by the actress Johanne Dybwad, who died at the age of 83 in 1950. In her youth she had played Ibsen's passionate women under his own critical eyes, and she was given the highest award any Norwegian can gain, the Grand Cross of St. Olav. She bore the broad red ribbon over her breast, not only as a reward for her own dazzling achievements but also as a mark of esteem for Norwegian dramatic art, which in her time had grown from its first stumbling efforts to full maturity.

We now come to the notes in more general use, the fives and the tens. Fridtjof Nansen's portrait is on the former. How shall we characterise this great son of Norway? Even so many years after his death in 1930 it is curiously difficult to summarize him, so versatile was he. During his lifetime he typified all that was distinguished, democratic, enterprising and dauntless. Nansen, who held a degree in zoology, was a remarkable sportsman and explorer: he crossed Greenland on skis, choosing the east-west route from which there was no turning back. He equipped the first "Fram" polar expedition and led it himself towards the North Pole, that glittering Fata Morgana which has tempted so many ill-fated men. He did not reach his goal, but came nearer to it than any man before him. He made an attempt to reach the Pole on foot, and his books describing these winters spent in the regions of eternal ice and snow have been read the world over. Nansen was an able spokesman for his country in the political crisis with Sweden in 1905, and after the First World War he devoted himself to the relief of suffering among the countless refugees, with an unflagging energy which won him the respect of the entire civilised world. He was the League of Nations' High Commissioner for the aid of refugees and prisoners, and at one time a passport with his name on it was sufficient to secure displaced persons certain basic civic rights.

His noble mind, his splendid physique and his eloquence gave him such a position in the eyes of all men that no title has ever been attached to his name. He is *Nansen* to the world.

The face on the 10-kroner notes is that of the politician Christian Michelsen, our leading figure in 1905, a most important date in our history. This was a year of crisis for Norway, and Norwegians had good reason to breathe a sigh of relief when it was safely behind them.

So long as the Union with Sweden lasted, our Storting fought a continual struggle to repeal the laws which stamped Norway as the inferior of the two countries. At the outset, in 1814, we were undoubtedly a good deal poorer and weaker than Sweden, but gradually, as prosperity grew under the leadership of wise political leaders, we began to feel we could well do without Swedish guardianship. At first we had a Swedish viceroy, but we found this irksome and the arrangement was of short duration.

The conflict about the national flags has already been mentioned; this ended with the passing of a law, without the royal assent, establishing the validety of the "true" Norwegian flag. The will of the people, expressed through the medium of the Storting, had at its third reading passed this law on its own authority.

But the consular service was another bone of contention. Norway wished to have her own representatives abroad, not to share her consuls with Sweden. It would have been preferable to have our own foreign minister, but that was unthought of at the time. The Storting voted that we should have our own consuls; the King refused to sign the bill, even when the Storting passed it for the third time, and his will prevailed.

The King, though old and sick, still presided over his own state council in Stockholm. At that time Norway had two prime ministers, one who led the Government at home and one in attendance on the King in Stockholm. The Norwegian minister in Sweden in 1905 was Jørgen Løvland, and he warned the King of the grave consequences his obstinacy might have. Oscar II still withheld his signature. Løvland then informed him that neither he nor any other Norwegian would ratify the King's decision, that the Government would inevitably resign, and that it would be impossible for the King to call together a new Government willing to carry out his decrees. Anyone who dared to support his resolutions would be accused by the Storting of disloyalty to the State and would be tried for treason. According to the Constitution the King, besides his own signature, required that of a Prime Minister, and if the minister refused to sign, the proposal could not become law.

The Storting met; the Prime Minister, Christian Michelsen, announced that the Government had tendered its resignation and that no new government had been formed. The President of the Storting, Carl Berner, put forward a resolution that was passed without debate: "Since all the members of the Cabinet have laid down their offices and His Majesty the King has declared himself unable to form a new Government for the country, and since, consequently, Royal Constitutional Power has ceased to function, the Storting authorises .... etc., etc."

The die was cast! The King had to have a Government, and if he could not provide one he was no longer King. It was a drastic conclusion, in fact parliamentary government at its most uncompromising. But Norwegians applauded this strong stand, for it was impressive, and, moreover, highly effective. The Swedes, on the other hand, considered the whole episode an insult to their nation, and a breach of respect towards their King. And we must admit, from the distance of half a century, that they had good reason to think so: it was, seen from any angle, a high-handed procedure to depose a King in a subordinate clause!

Powerful elements among the Swedish people were now in favour of declaring war against Norway, and the situation looked decidedly threatening. But the Swedish Labour Party held back, and so too did the old King. The great European powers were equally opposed to war, but their sympathies were unmistakably on the side of Sweden. They regarded the Norwegians as troublemakers, and, naturally enough, the Swedish view was better known abroad than the Norwegian, all foreign representatives being Swedish. It was at this point that Nansen came forward and pleaded with the world for the justice of Norway's claim. He succeeded in obtaining a hearing, particularly in England, where his popularity was already established.

It was an unprecedented situation: Norway regarded the Union as dissolved, whereas Sweden considered it to be still in force. The Swedes demanded a plebiscite on the question, and the Norwegian people went to the polls. In the whole of Norway there were only 184 men who voted for a continuance of the Union!

The summer of 1905 was tensely exciting, the

feeling among the people fluctuating between jubilation and apprehension. Negotiations with Sweden began in the autumn, and Christian Michelsen succeeded in bringing them to a happy conclusion. His countrymen were deeply grateful that the conflict was amicably settled, and his home town Bergen has erected a statue in his honour, where he stands, a typical Norwegian, his hand in his trouser pocket.

The Storting invited a Danish prince to come to Norway to be their King. Prince Carl replied, with the consideration and integrity which were typical of him, that he wished a plebiscite to be taken first, to ascertain whether the country wished for a monarchy or a republic. His father-in-law, King Edward VII of England, urged him to act quickly and decisively, but Prince Carl was of another mind: he waited until the result of the plebiscite showed an overwhelming majority in favour of the monarchy.

Prince Carl took the title of Haakon VII and, one snowy winter's day, he stepped for the first time onto Norwegian soil, his infant son Olav on his arm, Queen Maud by his side. It was Christian Michelsen who bade them welcome to their new country.

A new era had dawned for Norway. At long last we were again a free country and a free people, and we tried in every way to erase the memory of our years of bondage. We celebrated the centenary of our capital by changing its name from Christiania to the original medieval Oslo. We preferred to think of Oslo as Harald Hardrada's work rather than that of Christian IV. Of the old town, the Oslo which was ravaged by fire in 1624, there are few traces left.

Never at any stage has the nobility played any leading part in our history. At the national assembly at Eidsvoll in 1814 it was voted that no new titles and privileges should be granted; Christian Magnus Falsen proposed the total abolition of the nobility, declaring that he himself would give up all his own rights and privileges as a nobleman. He found no support at the time, and a fellow member somewhat maliciously wrote: "Falsen is now no longer a nobleman, but he saw to it that everybody knew he had *been* one".

Falsen did not have to wait long. In 1821 the Storting, with no opposition, abolished the nobility in Norway. Those of noble birth were, however, allowed to retain the title during their lifetime, and if they married their wives could bear the title that was their due. The nobility was slow in dying in Norway. Our last baron married late in life, and his baroness died more than a century after the abolition of the nobility.

The history of the Labour Party in Norway goes back to the time of the February Rising, when waves of revolutionary feeling swept in an irresistible tide from France to wash the shores of other lands. Marcus Thrane founded the first labour society in Drammen, and the movement spread quickly. Thrane drew up an appeal to the King, demanding social reforms such as general conscription and general suffrage. According to the prevailing law it was largely the poor who were conscripted and the wealthy who were privileged to vote. 13 000 men signed Thrane's appeal, but nevertheless it was rejected. Riots broke out, the leaders were thrown into prison, and Thrane was condemned to four years' hard labour. His was not the strong and steadfast character the situation demanded, and his tragedy lay, not so much in the injustice that he suffered, but in the fact that the movement required a stronger and tougher leader than he proved to be. He emigrated to America, where he died, but his ashes have been brought home by his countrymen and are interred in the churchyard in Oslo where the bones of our great men lie.

Only after a long struggle and many misunderstandings did the Labour movement in Norway win over the majority of electors and a Labour government came to power. The classical division of parties, between "Right" and «Left», conservative and radical, prevailed during the whole of the last century. In our day the situation has become more complicated, for we have 6 different political parties, though we have had a Labour Government since 1935.

In this century too we have had writers who have gained the attention and admiration of the world. Sigrid Undset and Knut Hamsun, both novelists of great talent, have, like Bjørnson, been awarded the Nobel Prize.

In the world of music Edvard Grieg won international fame, and was doubly appreciated by his proud countrymen because he drew his inspiration from our folk melodies. He was a great patriot and nature-lover, and one of the generation of happy wanderers who discovered our mountain wonderland.

Many of our painters have glorified the magnificent scenery of our country, but the most famous of them all is nevertheless Edvard Munch, who found his subjects in the human mind, in colour values and emotional depth. Neither he nor Gustav Vigeland, the sculptor, can be called "national" artists; their art is too strongly personal, and yet it has had a powerful influence on the generation of artists that followed them.

One of the most rugged personalities in the first half of the present century is Roald Amundsen, the man who reached both the South and the North Pole. He was the first man to accomplish the feat of sailing through the North-West Passage. The voyage took him three years in his ship "Gjøa" which measured 70 feet and carried a crew of eight. The scientific observations carried out by the expedition helped to throw fresh light on the magnetic North Pole.

Amundsen equipped a North Pole expedition to sail with Nansen's ship "Fram", but to the astonishment of the world he steered a course for the South, anchored off the edge of the barrier ice, and drove his huskies right to the Pole. This was in 1911, a bare month before the Englishman Scott reached the same goal in the tragic expedition which cost him his life.

For four years Amundsen struggled with the elements in the Arctic in a vain attempt to reach the North Pole, in a ship named "Maud" in honour of the Queen. But Amundsen would not give up: with the same indefatigable courage he defied both his backers and the arctic conditions, and in 1925 he started off with two planes, in an attempt to reach the North Pole by air. He did not achieve this goal, but he penetrated farther north than any other man before him. Yet he was not satisfied, and having succeeded in winning interest for his projects in Italy, in 1926, together with the Italian general Nobile, he flew over the North Pole in the airship "Norge". But the American, Byrd, had made a crossing by air only three days before!

General Nobile and Amundsen, two strong personalities, were unlikely to remain on good terms for long. Two years later Nobile reached the North Pole with an expedition of his own, but his airship "Italia" crashed and some of his men were lost. Asked to lead a rescue party, Amundsen consented without hesitation. In the French plane "Latham" he flew north in the search for the "Italia", but apparently the plane met with an accident three hours after starting, and Amundsen, with another Norwegian and the French crew of four, met his death in the Arctic waste.

Roald Amundsen was a re- markable man, both in temper- ament and appearance. His hawklike profile was easy to draw, and the boys of the time used to sketch Amund- sen's characteristic features in the margin of their school- books — a most convincing proof of his popularity.

Our country took no part in the First World War, in spite of the many attempts made to im- plicate us. Many of our seamen paid for the high freights with their lives, when ships were blown up by mines or sunk by U-boats during the North Sea blocade. For in Norway at that time, Pompeius' proud exhortation to the sailors twenty centuries ago, carrying corn to starving Rome, was a very present reality: "Navigare necesse est, vivere non est necesse". It is more important to sail than to live.

The wounds we suffered in the First World War are now but scars. But we are reminded of them when we see the mines which were set up as collecting boxes in our towns for the relief of seamen's widows and children.

In Norway, too, the post-war years, before Hitler became our common enemy, were a period of poli- tical and economic insecurity. He had his admirers in our country too, but they were few. Their leader, Vidkun Quisling, had never been a successful poli- tical leader. We watched with growing anxiety Hitler's progress, but that he would one day actually engulf our country too was altogether beyond belief. We would not, and could not, accept the possibility of such a disaster. There had not been war in Norway for well over a century, and to be embroiled in warfare was the last thing we wanted. In our simplicity, we believed our wish would be respected.

The Second World War began; Poland was defeated, Russia attacked Finland. Then came an episode in Norway which attracted much attention at the time:

A German transport, the "Altmark", with 300 British prisoners on board, came into Norwegian waters. It was detected by the British Navy, and the destroyer "Cossack" opened fire on the German ship in Norwegian territorial waters, boarded her and set the prisoners free. Two small Norwegian naval vessels were present; they lodged a protest but remained passive throughout the encounter. There is no question but that the sympathy of the Norwegians was on the side of the British, but neither was there any doubt that the captain of the "Cossack" had violated Norwegian neutrality, an inexcusable action under international law. The Germans used this episode as a convenient justification for their attack on Norway two months later. The encounter took place in the Jøssing Fjord in Southern Norway, and later our Nazi party used the name of "Jøssing" as a term of contempt for their adversaries. But Norwegians adopted the name for themselves and used it as a proud title.

During the five years of occupation the people of Norway were divided into two parties, "quislings" and "jøssings".

On the 9th of April, 1940, German warships steamed into all our most important ports and armed troops were landed. But their army of occupation did not escape without loss from its assault: the cruiser "Blücher" was sunk in the Oslo Fjord, and a naval battle took place at Narvik. British and French troops were landed, and the Norwegians joined forces with them under the command of General Ruge. It was a brief struggle against overwhelming odds; the King, the Crown Prince, the Storting and the Government made their hazardous way north to the districts still unoccupied, but on June 7th the King was obliged to leave his country, on board the British cruiser "Devonshire". It became apparent that further resistance was impossible, and when our allies had embarked, all military operations were abandoned.

The German occupation lasted five years, five long years. Compared with other countries overrun by German forces we did not suffer excessively: in accordance with his theory of the superiority of the Aryan race, Hitler felt obliged to set us up in a place of honour beside his own people, Scandinavians being even more Aryan than Germans, more Nordic, purer of stock. We were therefore to be respected as racial brothers, a situation which held little appeal for us.

It was impossible for the Germans to keep an

effective watch on our long coast-line; neither was it possible to guard the long Swedish border. It was hazardous, but not impossible, to leave occupied Norway during the war, and the escape routes were well organized. Boats ran regularly between Western Norway and the Shetlands, this route being popularly referred to as "The Shetland Bus". A man hunted by the Gestapo could be sure of finding friends everywhere. In spite of hardship, a strong sense of humour and neighbourliness enabled us to bear the cares and toil of the war years with greather stoicism than we should have thought possible. Arrests and imprisonment were daily occurrences, the prison camps in our country were filled to overflowing, and boat-loads of prisoners were sent to Germany. Hostages were taken, patriots shot.

Our forces in Great Britain were given the opportunity of taking part in raids on our own shores, and fought with distinction at Walcheren in Holland in 1944. But our greatest active war effort was that of the Merchant Service, which sailed the seven seas throughout the war, and of our Royal Navy, which helped to protect the transports, and crowned their achievements by the conspicuous part played in the landings on the Normandy coast on D-day, without the loss of a single vessel.

Many a tale could be told of courageous men and women, of traitors and informers, of buildings that were burned by Germans or destroyed by our friends and allies aiming at military targets. The entire northernmost district of Norway, Finnmark, suffered under the "scorched earth" policy when the Germans evacuated in fear of Russian invasion.

There are many whose names deserve mention, but one should be singled out — the poet Nordahl Grieg, shot down during a raid over Berlin when flying as a press observer. He had an active, eager mind which found its highest expression during the war, and his poems were smuggled home and spread throughout Norway, an inspiration to the young people in the war years. It is curious to note that of all the poems written in honour of King Haakon, the finest were by Communists. And Nordahl Grieg was among them.

The peace-loving old King Haakon proved to be a man of steel during those years, and the popularity he enjoyed was enormous. Even those who had voted for a republic in 1905 wished for nothing better than to see King Haakon once more back on Norwegian soil.

On the 7th June, 1945, five years to the day after the King's departure, the Royal family returned home on the cruiser "Norfolk". The British ensign which the "Norfolk" flew that day, now hangs in Nidaros Cathedral in Trondheim, our national shrine.

What have we achieved since the war years? We have built up again what was destroyed; our coastal towns, Molde, Kristiansund and all the northern towns are new — raised again from their ruins. They all have a similar architectural style, but little historic continuity. Much more has been built up than was destroyed, for in our country too the standard of living is rising and the lower classes of society are no longer content to live in crowded rooms — a development to rejoice over.

If a higher standard of living is a sign of a higher cultural level, we are making rapid progress. We can point proudly to many institutions and organisations which care for the old and sick, and for those who will carry the burdens of future responsibility on their shoulders.

Nevertheless, there are still romantics amongst us to whom the past means almost as much as the future, and who take pleasure in tracing our civilisation back through the centuries. You must be one of them, for otherwise you would not have read this book!